Michael Hofmann was born in 1957 in Freiburg, Germany, and came to England in 1961. He has published four volumes of poems and won a Cholmondeley Award and the Geoffrey Memorial Prize for poetry. His translations have won many awards, including the *Independent*'s Foreign Fiction Award, the IMPAC Dublin Literary Award and the PEN Book-of-the-Month Club Translation Prize. His reviews and criticism are gathered in *Behind the Lines* (2001). He has recently edited *The Faber Book of 20th-Century German Poems* (2005)

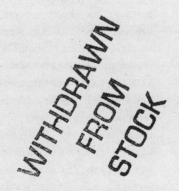

# ROBERT LOWELL
## Poems selected by
### MICHAEL HOFMANN

*faber and faber*

This selection first published in 2001
by Faber and Faber Limited
3 Queen Square London WC1N 3AU

This edition first published in 2006

Photoset by Parker Typesetting Service, Leicester
Printed in England by Bookmarque Ltd, Croydon, Surrey

Introduction and selection © Michael Hofmann, 2001
Poems © The Estate of Robert Lowell, 1959, 1964, 1967, 1969,
1973, 1976, 2001

The right of Michael Hofmann to be identified as the
editor of this work has been asserted in accordance with
Section 77 of the Copyright, Designs and Patents Act 1988

A CIP record for this book
is available from the British Library

ISBN 0-571-23040-7

10 9 8 7 6 5 4 3 2 1

# Contents

# Introduction

'*Ich sitze und lese einen Dichter*,' Rilke has Malte his alter ego say in *The Notebook of Malte Laurids Brigge*, 'Here I sit, reading a poet.' And then he has him look about him in the Bibliothèque Nationale in Paris, and wonder, not very hard, what everyone else can be reading.

Malte's choice of word is illuminating. One reads novels, stories, plays – but one reads *a poet*. The singular and the personal, and the suggestion of privilege, are right. At a certain pitch of expectation, there are not many possibilities. 'There are not three hundred poets,' says Malte. (In the case of living poets, there's a simple test: whose books do you wait for? It's never very many. Of the rest, there may be some that are agreeable surprises, or that don't hurt – but what's that matter?) George Steiner asks 'Tolstoy or Dostoevsky', but it's really a poetry question, and would make more sense asked about poets. Eliot or Stevens? Larkin or Hughes? Benn or Brecht? Pasternak or Mandelstam, if you want it in Russian. In prose, you just take them both, and dab your lips with your napkin. Prose is inclusive; poetry is exclusive. It's not really a question of competition, of the notorious competitiveness of poets. Poetry by its nature reduces, sharpens, distills, compresses; 'Dichten = condensare' noted Bunting, following Pound. Choosing a poet is a further degree of reduction, sharpening, distillation, compression. As such, it doesn't much resemble other forms of choosing – from menus, in a voting booth, with anguish or equanimity, with a pin or a zapper. Hence the frequently observed phenomenon of feeling chosen by a poet as much as choosing. 'Here I sit, reading a poet.'

For many people, on both sides of the Atlantic, the pre-eminent poet in what was called the mid-century – the 1950s to the 1970s – was Robert Lowell. It is a little strange to think of now, when there are arguably no great careers in progress in the United States, and little work of distinction is being produced; when various claims and counter-claims to the contrary seem equally unpersuasive; and when Lowell himself has somewhat fallen on hard times ('like, do people still *read* Robert Lowell?' an American student said to me – even so, one who had at least heard of him); but he held that exposed, singular, prototypical and privileged position, probably from 1947, when he was thirty and his first trade book *Lord.Weary's Castle* won the Pulitzer, to 1977, when his last, *Day by Day*, was published posthumously.

Lowell's standing as a poet was never a straightforward matter: it was always vexed by the social distinction of his background, the commotion of his life, the controversies that sprang up around his work at various times, the startling vehemence, at all times, of his supporters and opponents. 'There is no other poetry today quite like this' (Tate), 'Robert Lowell is probably the most distinguished American poet of his generation' (Hollander), 'one can prophesy that his next book will establish his name as that normally thought of for "the" American poet' (Ehrenpreis), 'Robert Lowell is, by something like critical consensus, the greatest American poet of the mid-century, probably the greatest poet now writing in English' (Poirier). Lowell was not yet fifty when Ehrenpreis's essay came out, entitled 'The Age of Lowell' – and Ehrenpreis didn't mean 'not yet fifty' either. And yet, at the same time as these gauchely suave or suavely gauche accolades were being nailed or glued together, in other parts of the forest Lowell was being ritually shredded. Every successive book of his met with contumelious rejection, from people who had rejected him before, or from people who were new to the game. 'This book does little to add to Lowell's standing as a poet' (of *Life Studies*); 'most of the poems in *For the Union Dead* are bad poems'; 'the last [Lowell] the most discouraging of all, surviving to dissipate *Lord Weary's Castle* and nine subsequent useful poems in the seedy grandiloquence of *Notebook*.' (What, outside of Brecht or Mayakovsky, is a 'useful poem'?!) Still, at least these words from the flip-flopping Donald Hall proved to be 'useful criticism': Lowell cheekily accommodated them in the poem 'Last Night', in a further edition of *Notebook*. All this, finally, is put in context in a bizarre stricken ramble of a piece by another American poet, Hayden Carruth, who wrote:

> Robert Lowell is, and for some years has been, the most envied poet in the country. The consequences of this are many, but for the moment I wish simply to enforce the fact. I envy Lowell. Everywhere I go among literary people I meet only others who envy Lowell. [. . .] Envy is a tricky thing, of course. It takes many directions. At bottom it accounts, I believe, for ninety percent of the critical response to Lowell's work, the wide range of opinions, and it accounts too for the concentration of responses at the extremes of the scale: adulators at one end, detractors at the other.

This is extraordinary, even alarming, but I see no reason not to believe it.

One might have expected these personality-driven issues to have receded after Lowell's death, leaving the poetry there to be read, but it hasn't happened that way. Rather, the climate has remained hostile, unforgiving, unenlightened – and instead, Elizabeth Bishop has been discovered in a big way. Obviously, the former has been a bad thing for Lowell's posthumous reputation, but I think his British readership has also been affected by it – not least from not even understanding the particular cloud under which Lowell continued to find himself. It begins with 'Lowell' and 'Boston', the fabled world where 'the Cabots talked only to the Lowells, and the Lowells talked only to God', of illustrious and secure and prosperous families going back for generations. In England, where social distinction is far more plentiful and arguably counts for far less, it is hard to get any sense of how this background could be overplayed and resented by Lowell's unsympathetic readers and rivals in America. They chose, too, to overhear the dry, deprecating humour with which Lowell presented such material, as for instance, in the opening of his prose piece 'Antebellum Boston', with its nod at Henry Adams: 'I, too, was born under the shadow of the Boston State House, and under Pisces, the fish, on the first of March 1917.' (Interestingly, it took an English reviewer of *Life Studies*, namely Stephen Spender, to remark on 'a very great and idiosyncratic humour' that is indeed one of the magnificent things about the book.) Even the more comprehending and well-disposed envy of Elizabeth Bishop seems to me misconceived:

> I feel that I could write in as much detail about my Uncle Artie, say, but what would be the significance? Nothing at all. [. . .] Whereas all you have to do is put down the names! And the fact that it seems significant, illustrative, American, etc., gives you, I think, the confidence you display about tackling any idea or theme, *seriously*, in both writing and conversation.

This seems to me to be taking a qualitative but effectively neutral difference for a quantitative one. There is more than enough room for both Uncle Artie and Uncle Devereux. Lineage by itself counts for nothing in poetry.

Roughly adjacent to this matter of birth and privilege is a certain grandiosity in the conduct of Lowell's life, and a flair for gesture. (Of course, publicity as it is known to us did not exist when Lowell was alive, but I feel he would have been quite good at it; meanwhile, the crude imputation of publicity-seeking misrepresents his character and achievements about as badly as anything can.) I refer to such things as his conversion to Catholicism as a young man, his quitting Harvard for Kenyon, his conscientious objection to the War (for which he had previously volunteered) and subsequent brief term in gaol, his refusal of Lyndon Johnson's invitation to the White House, his friendships with Jackie Kennedy and

Eugene McCarthy, his participation in the peace marches of the Sixties (diligently and creepily chronicled by Norman Mailer in his *Armies of the Night*). His marriages and divorces and bereavements, the cycles of mania and depression he endured more or less annually from about 1960, even such on the face of it inconsequential things as his regular summers in Maine, his leaving Boston for New York City, and New York City for London, all are heavily and clearly marked in his work, and give it its epic, systolic quality. This is simply what happens with poets, they write about what it is in their gift to write about, and over time this imprints itself on their writing, and hence on their readers. If Lowell's life seems large, it is not large in a different way than, say, Yeats's, or MacNeice's, or Brodsky's.

This leads me to the third impediment to a fair or fresh reading of Lowell: the fact that – it's quite a rarity for a poet – he got in trouble not once, but several times, for the way he wrote. *Life Studies* shows important continuities with what went before, but mainly it marks a great change of direction for a poet previously known for his dramatic monologues, his apocalyptic imagery, his thumping rhythms, his couplets and his sublime, impersonal authority. Inevitably, it alienated a sizeable part of his following. The part that liked it found themselves alienated, not long afterwards, by a book called *Near the Ocean*, an expensive production, with illustrations by Sidney Nolan, which incorporated adaptations from the Classics, satirical elements, and heavy use of rhymed octosyllabics. When he followed this with a book of unrhymed 14-line poems ('sonnets') called variously *Notebook*, *Notebook of a Year* and *Notebook 1967–68*, which he kept revising and expanding until it finally split into two books called *History* and *For Lizzie and Harriet* which he brought out on the same day (in June 1973) as yet another book of 'sonnets' called *The Dolphin*, readers and critics had some reason to feel exasperated. In particular, his use as poems of personal letters addressed to him by Elizabeth

Hardwick, his second wife, was felt to be intolerable. Against this, I would argue that it is a better thing (remember Malte) for a poet to suffer from excessive variety than excessive similarity or self-conformity; that there is something quite exhilarating about making one's way through the books of 14-line poems of the late 60s and early 70s, which resemble a standard book of poems about as much as a jungle resembles a bunch of flowers; and that while the use of letters was a breach of trust, it was not done for any 'life-reasons' – either vindictively, or to look good himself – but out of a misapplied and characteristic and excessive belief in the importance of poetry.

If none of these – the range, the 'sonnets', the use of letters – have been properly addressed and dismissed, nor has what I would call the C-word, 'Confessionalism', a term coined in 1960 by the critic M. L. Rosenthal, and used more or less unthinkingly and sloppily ever since. Ambitious and conscious and artful poems like Lowell's mock such an appellation. The degree to which they presume on the reader's human involvement with their subject matter is negligible. They do not serve prurience by dishing up a stream of private and discreditable things. Poets, it seems to me, have always written like Lowell – 'from life' – and the interest is not in the material, but in what is made of it. '*Das Gedichtete behauptet sein Recht, wie das Geschehene,*' insisted Goethe, there is a truth and a justice in poetry, as much as there is in history. It is an unhappy sign of our times that we are apt to put our own levelling construction upon things, to take an inadequate paraphrase for a poem, to go for garish notions of content, to trust – or vilify – the teller, not the tale.

This fails to take account of anything done in language: it treats all language as equal and irrelevant. Lowell, though, it seems to me, wrote facing the language, and with an unprecedented and unequalled plasticity of language: 'lines, words, letters nailed to letters, words, lines –/ the typescript looks like a Rosetta Stone.' When he writes, 'Crows maunder on the petrified fairway,' I can't be persuaded that he is doing anything as transparent and secondary and subservient as confessing: it's the 'w's that interest him, and the diphthongs, the submerged 'foul' or 'fowl', the priceless velleity of 'maunder' in glacially slow time. Equally, when he writes: 'These are the tranquillized *Fifties*,/ and I am forty,' it does not bespeak a social – a class – confidence, but a gift with a phrase, an ear for internal rhyme, an ability to surprise, a lifelong sympathy with the slothful and laggardly, a poet's willingness to connect the inner with the outer – or, here, something like the inside of the outside, and the outside of the inside – and considerable early practice with 'and', gained in the course of many years of writing in pentameter. There is a charmed and inexhaustible amplitude in his writing which has kept me going back to it ever since I first read it, as an undergraduate, in 1976.

If this short selection of his poetry accomplishes anything, then I hope it will bring new readers to his work, as I myself was brought then by the omnibus printing of *Life Studies* and *For the Union Dead* that I borrowed from a friend. I was still pronouncing his name as though it rhymed with 'towel' or 'vowel'. By the time I trained myself in the 'Noel' pronunciation, and had given the book back, I learned that Lowell had died. Truly, one doesn't need to know anything more than Malte knew. After all, what is it that makes a poet? Interest, distinctiveness, trustworthiness; the ability to make himself heard through his lines when the poet himself or herself is long dead and gone; the assiduousness and resourcefulness with which he has been able to process his life and times into poems; his qualities as a companion to us, in our lives and our times; the sense that, try as we may, we will never be finished with reading him. This is what matters about Robert Lowell, not the fact that he may have lorded it – intentionally or not – over his contemporaries, or the other trivialities of his reputation, some of them listed above.

I have chosen not to include any of the poems before *Life*

*Studies*, not because I hate them, but because I don't love any of them as much, and because none of them is as propulsive as 'Beyond the Alps', the poem with which *Life Studies* begins. If the reader feels similarly propelled; or acquires a taste for the 'sonnets' that make up half the pages here; or goes on to read the *Collected Poems* and the *Letters* – both of them, I believe, imminent – I will be happy. To my mind, Lowell put words together as compellingly as anyone in English in the twentieth century; along with Benn and Montale, he is one of its great voices: like them, he understood that the modern poem is all about vocal quality, '*monologisch*' in Benn's word. He applied Pound's invention, logopoiea, to a prose diction, and wrote lines – when he had a mind to – as mighty as Marlowe's. 'I am not sure whether I can distinguish between intention and interpretation,' he wrote deprecatingly once, when confronted with several expert readings of 'Skunk Hour' – and then, astutely, greedily, immodestly, accurately: 'I think this is what I more or less intended.'

Michael Hofmann

# ROBERT LOWELL

## Beyond the Alps

*(On the train from Rome to Paris. 1950, the year when Pius XII
defined the dogma of Mary's bodily assumption.)*

Reading how even the Swiss had thrown the sponge
in once again and Everest was still
unscaled, I watched our Paris pullman lunge
mooning across the fallow Alpine snow.
*O bella Roma!* I saw our stewards go
forward on tiptoe banging on their gongs.
Man changed to landscape. Much against my will,
I left the City of God where it belongs.
There the skirt-mad Mussolini unfurled
the eagle of Caesar. He was one of us
only, pure prose. I envy the conspicuous
waste of our grandparents on their grand tours –
long-haired Victorian sages accepted the universe,
while breezing on their trust funds through the world.

When the Vatican made Mary's Assumption dogma,
the crowds at San Pietro screamed *Papa*.
The Holy Father dropped his shaving glass,
and listened. His electric razor purred,
his pet canary chirped on his left hand.
The lights of science couldn't hold a candle
to Mary risen – at one miraculous stroke,
angel-wing'd, gorgeous as a jungle bird!
But who believed this? Who could understand?
Pilgrims still kissed Saint Peter's brazen sandal.
The Duce's lynched, bare, booted skull still spoke.
God herded his people to the *coup de grâce* –
the costumed Switzers sloped their pikes to push,
O Pius, through the monstrous human crush. . . .

Our mountain-climbing train had come to earth.
Tired of the querulous hush-hush of the wheels,

3

the blear-eyed ego kicking in my berth
lay still, and saw Apollo plant his heels
on terra firma through the morning's thigh . . .
each backward, wasted Alp, a Parthenon,
fire-branded socket of the Cyclop's eye.
There are no tickets for that altitude
once held by Hellas, when the Goddess stood,
prince, pope, philosopher and golden bough,
pure mind and murder at the scything prow –
Minerva, the miscarriage of the brain.

Now Paris, our black classic, breaking up
like killer kings on an Etruscan cup.

# A Mad Negro Soldier Confined at Munich

'We're all Americans, except the Doc,
a Kraut DP, who kneels and bathes my eye.
The boys who floored me, two black maniacs, try
to pat my hands. Rounds, rounds! Why punch the clock?

In Munich the zoo's rubble fumes with cats;
hoydens with air-guns prowl the Koenigsplatz,
and pink the pigeons on the mustard spire.
Who but my girl-friend set the town on fire?

Cat-houses talk cold turkey to my guards;
I found my *Fraulein* stitching outing shirts
in the black forest of the colored wards –
lieutenants squawked like chickens in her skirts.

Her German language made my arteries harden –
I've no annuity from the pay we blew.
I chartered an aluminium canoe,
I had her six times in the English Garden.

Oh mama, mama, like a trolley-pole
sparkling at contact, her electric shock –
the power-house! . . . The doctor calls our roll –
no knives, no forks. We file before the clock,

and fancy minnows, slaves of habit, shoot
like starlight through their air-conditioned bowl.
It's time for feeding. Each subnormal boot-
black heart is pulsing to its ant-egg dole.'

# Ford Madox Ford

(1873–1939)

The lobbed ball plops, then dribbles to the cup. . . .
(a birdie Fordie!) But it nearly killed
the ministers. Lloyd George was holding up
the flag. He gabbled, 'Hop-toad, hop-toad, hop-toad!
Hueffer has used a niblick on the green;
it's filthy art, Sir, filthy art!'
You answered, 'What is art to me and thee?
Will a blacksmith teach a midwife how to bear?'
That cut the puffing statesman down to size,
Ford. You said, 'Otherwise,
I would have been general of a division.' Ah Ford!
Was it war, the sport of kings, that your *Good Soldier*,
the best French novel in the language, taught
those Georgian Whig magnificoes at Oxford,
at Oxford decimated on the Somme?
Ford, five times black-balled for promotion,
then mustard gassed voiceless some seven miles
behind the lines at Nancy or Belleau Wood:
you emerged in your 'worn uniform,
gilt dragons on the revers of the tunic,'
a Jonah – O divorced, divorced
from the whale-fat of post-war London! Boomed,
cut, plucked and booted! In Provence, New York . . .
marrying, blowing . . . nearly dying
at Boulder, when the altitude
pressed the world on your heart,
and your audience, almost football-size,
shrank to a dozen, while you stood
mumbling, with fish-blue eyes,
and mouth pushed out
fish-fashion, as if you gagged for air. . . .
Sandman! Your face, a childish *O*. The sun

is pernod-yellow and it gilds the heirs
of all the ages there on Washington
and Stuyvesant, your Lilliputian squares,
where writing turned your pockets inside out.
But master, mammoth mumbler, tell me why
the bales of your left-over novels buy
less than a bandage for your gouty foot.
Wheel-horse, O unforgetting elephant,
I hear you huffing at your old Brevoort,
Timon and Falstaff, while you heap the board
for publishers. Fiction! I'm selling short
your lies that made the great your equals. Ford,
you were a kind man and you died in want.

## Terminal Days at Beverly Farms

At Beverly Farms, a portly, uncomfortable boulder
bulked in the garden's centre –
an irregular Japanese touch.
After his Bourbon 'old fashioned,' Father,
bronzed, breezy, a shade too ruddy,
swayed as if on deck-duty
under his six pointed star-lantern –
last July's birthday present.
He smiled his oval Lowell smile,
he wore his cream gabardine dinner-jacket,
and indigo cummerbund.
His head was efficient and hairless,
his newly dieted figure was vitally trim.

Father and Mother moved to Beverly Farms
to be a two minute walk from the station,
half an hour by train from the Boston doctors.
They had no sea-view,
but sky-blue tracks of the commuters' railroad shone
like a double-barrelled shotgun
through the scarlet late August sumac,
multiplying like cancer
at their garden's border.

Father had had two coronaries.
He still treasured underhand economies,
but his best friend was his little black *Chevie*,
garaged like a sacrificial steer
with gilded hooves,
yet sensationally sober,
and with less side than an old dancing pump.
The local dealer, a 'buccaneer',
had been bribed a 'king's ransom'
to quickly deliver a car without chrome.

Each morning at eight-thirty,
inattentive and beaming,
loaded with his 'calc' and 'trig' books,
his clipper ship statistics,
and his ivory slide rule,
Father stole off with the *Chevie*
to loaf in the Maritime Museum at Salem.
He called the curator
'the commander of the Swiss Navy'.

Father's death was abrupt and unprotesting.
His vision was still twenty-twenty.
After a morning of anxious, repetitive smiling,
his last words to Mother were:
'I feel awful.'

## Father's Bedroom

In my Father's bedroom:
blue threads as thin
as pen writing on the bedspread,
blue dots on the curtains,
a blue kimono,
Chinese sandals with blue plush straps.
The broad-planked floor
had a sandpapered neatness.
The clear glass bed-lamp
with a white doily shade
was still raised a few
inches by resting on volume two
of Lafcadio Hearn's
*Glimpses of unfamiliar Japan*.
Its warped olive cover
was punished like a rhinoceros hide.
In the flyleaf:
'Robbie from Mother.'
Years later in the same hand:
'This book has had hard usage
On the Yangtze River, China.
It was left under an open
porthole in a storm.'

# For Sale

Poor sheepish plaything,
organized with prodigal animosity,
lived in just a year –
my Father's cottage at Beverly Farms
was on the market the month he died.
Empty, open, intimate,
its town-house furniture
had an on tiptoe air
of waiting for the mover
on the heels of the undertaker.
Ready, afraid
of living alone till eighty,
Mother mooned in a window,
as if she had stayed on a train
one stop past her destination.

## Sailing Home from Rapallo

*(February 1954)*

Your nurse could only speak Italian,
but after twenty minutes I could imagine your final week,
and tears ran down my cheeks. . . .

When I embarked from Italy with my Mother's body,
the whole shoreline of the *Golfo di Genova*
was breaking into fiery flower.
The crazy yellow and azure sea-sleds
blasting like jack hammers across
the *spumante*-bubbling wake of our liner,
recalled the clashing colours of my Ford.
Mother travelled first-class in the hold,
her *Risorgimento* black and gold casket
was like Napoleon's at the *Invalides*. . . .

While the passengers were tanning
on the Mediterranean in deck-chairs,
our family cemetery in Dunbarton
lay under the White Mountains
in the sub-zero weather.
The graveyard's soil was changing to stone –
so many of its deaths had been midwinter.
Dour and dark against the blinding snowdrifts,
its black brook and fir trunks were as smooth as masts.
A fence of iron spear-hafts
black-bordered its mostly Colonial grave-slates.
The only 'unhistoric' soul to come here
was Father, now buried beneath his recent
unweathered pink-veined slice of marble.
Even the Latin of his Lowell motto:
*Occasionem cognosce,*
seemed too businesslike and pushing here,
where the burning cold illuminated

the hewn inscriptions of Mother's relatives:
twenty or thirty Winslows and Starks.
Frost had given their names a diamond edge. . . .

In the grandiloquent lettering on Mother's coffin,
*Lowell* had been misspelled *LOVEL*.
The corpse
was wrapped like *panetone* in Italian tinfoil.

# Waking in the Blue

The night attendant, a B.U. sophomore,
rouses from the mare's-nest of his drowsy head
propped on *The Meaning of Meaning*.
He catwalks down our corridor.
Azure day
makes my agonized blue window bleaker.
Crows maunder on the petrified fairway.
Absence! My heart grows tense
as though a harpoon were sparring for the kill.
(This is the house for the 'mentally ill'.)

What use is my sense of humour?
I grin at 'Stanley', now sunk in his sixties,
once a Harvard all-American fullback,
(if such were possible!)
still hoarding the build of a boy in his twenties,
as he soaks, a ramrod
with the muscle of a seal
in his long tub,
vaguely urinous from the Victorian plumbing.
A kingly granite profile in a crimson golf-cap,
worn all day, all night,
he thinks only of his figure,
of slimming on sherbet and ginger ale –
more cut off from words than a seal.

This is the way day breaks in Bowditch Hall at McLean's;
the hooded night lights bring out 'Bobbie',
Porcellian '29,
a replica of Louis XVI
without the wig –
redolent and roly-poly as a sperm whale,
as he swashbuckles about in his birthday suit
and horses at chairs.

These victorious figures of bravado ossified young.

In between the limits of day,
hours and hours go by under the crew haircuts
and slightly too little nonsensical bachelor twinkle
of the Roman Catholic attendants.
(There are no Mayflower
screwballs in the Catholic Church.)

After a hearty New England breakfast,
I weigh two hundred pounds
this morning. Cock of the walk,
I strut in my turtle-necked French sailor's jersey
before the metal shaving mirrors,
and see the shaky future grow familiar
in the pinched, indigenous faces
of these thoroughbred mental cases,
twice my age and half my weight.
We are all old-timers,
each of us holds a locked razor.

# Home After Three Months Away

Gone now the baby's nurse,
a lioness who ruled the roost
and made the Mother cry.
She used to tie
gobbets of porkrind in bowknots of gauze –
three months they hung like soggy toast
on our eight foot magnolia tree,
and helped the English sparrows
weather a Boston winter.

Three months, three months!
Is Richard now himself again?
Dimpled with exaltation,
my daughter holds her levee in the tub.
Our noses rub,
each of us pats a stringy lock of hair –
they tell me nothing's gone.
Though I am forty-one,
not forty now, the time I put away
was child's play. After thirteen weeks
my child still dabs her cheeks
to start me shaving. When
we dress her in her sky-blue corduroy,
she changes to a boy,
and floats my shaving brush
and washcloth in the flush. . . .
Dearest, I cannot loiter here
in lather like a polar bear.

Recuperating, I neither spin nor toil.
Three stories down below,
a choreman tends our coffin's length of soil,
and seven horizontal tulips blow.
Just twelve months ago,

these flowers were pedigreed
imported Dutchmen, now no one need
distinguish them from weed.
Bushed by the late spring snow,
they cannot meet
another year's snowballing enervation.

I keep no rank nor station.
Cured, I am frizzled, stale and small.

# Memories of West Street and Lepke

Only teaching on Tuesdays, book-worming
in pyjamas fresh from the washer each morning,
I hog a whole house on Boston's
'hardly passionate Marlborough Street',
where even the man
scavenging filth in the back alley trash cans,
has two children, a beach wagon, a helpmate,
and is 'a young Republican'.
I have a nine months' daughter,
young enough to be my granddaughter.
Like the sun she rises in her flame-flamingo infants' wear.

These are the tranquillized *Fifties*,
and I am forty. Ought I to regret my seedtime?
I was a fire-breathing Catholic C.O.,
and made my manic statement,
telling off the state and president, and then
sat waiting sentence in the bull pen
beside a negro boy with curlicues
of marijuana in his hair.

Given a year,
I walked on the roof of the West Street Jail, a short
enclosure like my school soccer court,
and saw the Hudson River once a day
through sooty clothesline entanglements
and bleaching khaki tenements.
Strolling, I yammered metaphysics with Abramowitz,
a jaundice-yellow ('it's really tan')
and fly-weight pacifist,
so vegetarian,
he wore rope shoes and preferred fallen fruit.
He tried to convert Bioff and Brown,
the Hollywood pimps, to his diet.

Hairy, muscular, suburban,
wearing chocolate double-breasted suits,
they blew their tops and beat him black and blue.

I was so out of things, I'd never heard
of the Jehovah's Witnesses.
'Are you a C.O.?' I asked a fellow jailbird.
'No,' he answered, 'I'm a J.W.'
He taught me the hospital 'tuck',
and pointed out the T-shirted back
of *Murder Incorporated's* Czar Lepke,
there piling towels on a rack,
or dawdling off to his little segregated cell full
of things forbidden the common man:
a portable radio, a dresser, two toy American
flags tied together with a ribbon of Easter palm.
Flabby, bald, lobotomized,
he drifted in a sheepish calm,
where no agonizing reappraisal
jarred his concentration on the electric chair –
hanging like an oasis in his air
of lost connections . . .

## Man and Wife

Tamed by *Miltown*, we lie on Mother's bed;
the rising sun in war paint dyes us red;
in broad daylight her gilded bed-posts shine,
abandoned, almost Dionysian.
At last the trees are green on Marlborough Street,
blossoms on our magnolia ignite
the morning with their murderous five days' white.
All night I've held your hand,
as if you had
a fourth time faced the kingdom of the mad —
its hackneyed speech, its homicidal eye —
and dragged me home alive. . . . Oh my *Petite*,
clearest of all God's creatures, still all air and nerve:
you were in your twenties, and I,
once hand on glass
and heart in mouth,
outdrank the Rahvs in the heat
of Greenwich Village, fainting at your feet —
too boiled and shy
and poker-faced to make a pass,
while the shrill verve
of your invective scorched the traditional South.

Now twelve years later, you turn your back.
Sleepless, you hold
your pillow to your hollows like a child,
your old-fashioned tirade —
loving, rapid, merciless —
breaks like the Atlantic Ocean on my head.

## 'To Speak of the Woe that Is in Marriage'

*'It is the future generation that presses into being by means of these exuberant feelings and supersensible soap bubbles of ours.'*

SCHOPENHAUER

'The hot night makes us keep our bedroom windows open.
Our magnolia blossoms. Life begins to happen.
My hopped up husband drops his home disputes,
and hits the streets to cruise for prostitutes,
free-lancing out along the razor's edge.
This screwball might kill his wife, then take the pledge.
Oh the monotonous meanness of his lust. . . .
It's the injustice . . . he is so unjust —
whiskey-blind, swaggering home at five.
My only thought is how to keep alive.
What makes him tick? Each night now I tie
ten dollars and his car key to my thigh. . . .
Gored by the climacteric of his want,
he stalls above me like an elephant.'

# Skunk Hour

*for Elizabeth Bishop*

Nautilus Island's hermit
heiress still lives through winter in her Spartan cottage;
her sheep still graze above the sea.
Her son's a bishop. Her farmer
is first selectman in our village,
she's in her dotage.

Thirsting for
the hierarchic privacy
of Queen Victoria's century,
she buys up all
the eyesores facing her shore,
and lets them fall.

The season's ill –
we've lost our summer millionaire,
who seemed to leap from an L. L. Bean
catalogue. His nine-knot yawl
was auctioned off to lobstermen.
A red fox stain covers Blue Hill.

And now our fairy
decorator brightens his shop for fall,
his fishnet's filled with orange cork,
orange, his cobbler's bench and awl,
there is no money in his work,
he'd rather marry.

One dark night,
my Tudor Ford climbed the hill's skull,
I watched for love-cars. Lights turned down,
they lay together, hull to hull,
where the graveyard shelves on the town. . . .
My mind's not right.

A car radio bleats,
'Love, O careless Love . . .' I hear
my ill-spirit sob in each blood cell,
as if my hand were at its throat . . .
I myself am hell,
nobody's here –

only skunks, that search
in the moonlight for a bite to eat.
They march on their soles up Main Street:
white stripes, moonstruck eyes' red fire
under the chalk-dry and spar spire
of the Trinitarian Church.

I stand on top
of our back steps and breathe the rich air –
a mother skunk with her column of kittens swills the garbage
    pail.
She jabs her wedge head in a cup
of sour cream, drops her ostrich tail,
and will not scare.

# Water

It was a Maine lobster town —
each morning boatloads of hands
pushed off for granite
quarries on the islands,

and left dozens of bleak
white frame houses stuck
like oyster shells
on a hill of rock,

and below us, the sea lapped
the raw little match-stick
mazes of a weir,
where the fish for bait were trapped.

Remember? We sat on a slab of rock.
From this distance in time,
it seems the color
of iris, rotting and turning purpler,

but it was only
the usual gray rock
turning the usual green
when drenched by the sea.

The sea drenched the rock
at our feet all day,
and kept tearing away
flake after flake.

One night you dreamed
you were a mermaid clinging to a wharf-pile,
and trying to pull
off the barnacles with your hands.

We wished our two souls
might return like gulls
to the rock. In the end,
the water was too cold for us.

# The Old Flame

My old flame, my wife!
Remember our lists of birds?
One morning last summer, I drove
by our house in Maine. It was still
on top of its hill —

Now a red ear of Indian maize
was splashed on the door.
Old Glory with thirteen stars
hung on a pole. The clapboard
was old-red schoolhouse red.

Inside, a new landlord,
a new wife, a new broom!
Atlantic seaboard antique shop
pewter and plunder
shone in each room.

A new frontier!
No running next door
now to phone the sheriff
for his taxi to Bath
and the State Liquor Store!

No one saw your ghostly
imaginary lover
stare through the window,
and tighten
the scarf at his throat.

Health to the new people,
health to their flag, to their old
restored house on the hill!
Everything had been swept bare,
furnished, garnished, and aired.

Everything's changed for the best –
how quivering and fierce we were,
there snowbound together,
simmering like wasps
in our tent of books!

Poor ghost, old love, speak
with your old voice
of flaming insight
that kept us awake all night.
In one bed and apart,

we heard the plow
groaning up hill –
a red light, then a blue,
as it tossed off the snow
to the side of the road.

# The Mouth of the Hudson

*for Esther Brooks*

A single man stands like a bird-watcher,
and scuffles the pepper and salt snow
from a discarded, gray
Westinghouse Electric cable drum.
He cannot discover America by counting
the chains of condemned freight-trains
from thirty states. They jolt and jar
and junk in the siding below him.
He has trouble with his balance.
His eyes drop,
and he drifts with the wild ice
ticking seaward down the Hudson,
like the blank sides of a jig-saw puzzle.

The ice ticks seaward like a clock.
A Negro toasts
wheat-seeds over the coke-fumes
of a punctured barrel.
Chemical air
sweeps in from New Jersey,
and smells of coffee.

Across the river,
ledges of suburban factories tan
in the sulphur-yellow sun
of the unforgivable landscape.

# Fall 1961

Back and forth, back and forth
goes the tock, tock, tock
of the orange, bland, ambassadorial
face of the moon
on the grandfather clock.

All autumn, the chafe and jar
of nuclear war;
we have talked our extinction to death.
I swim like a minnow
behind my studio window.

Our end drifts nearer,
the moon lifts,
radiant with terror.
The state
is a diver under a glass bell.

A father's no shield
for his child.
We are like a lot of wild
spiders crying together,
but without tears.

Nature holds up a mirror.
One swallow makes a summer.
It's easy to tick
off the minutes,
but the clockhands stick.

Back and forth!
Back and forth, back and forth –
my one point of rest
is the orange and black
oriole's swinging nest!

## Eye and Tooth

My whole eye was sunset red,
the old cut cornea throbbed,
I saw things darkly,
as through an unwashed goldfish globe.

I lay all day on my bed.
I chain-smoked through the night,
learning to flinch
at the flash of the matchlight.

Outside, the summer rain,
a simmer of rot and renewal,
fell in pinpricks.
Even new life is fuel.

My eyes throb.
Nothing can dislodge
the house with my first tooth
noosed in a knot to the doorknob.

Nothing can dislodge
the triangular blotch
of rot on the red roof,
a cedar hedge, or the shade of a hedge.

No ease from the eye
of the sharp-shinned hawk in the birdbook there,
with reddish-brown buffalo hair
on its shanks, one ascetic talon

clasping the abstract imperial sky.
It says:
*an eye for an eye,*
*a tooth for a tooth.*

No ease for the boy at the keyhole,
his telescope,
when the women's white bodies flashed
in the bathroom. Young, my eyes began to fail.

Nothing! No oil
for the eye, nothing to pour
on those waters or flames.
I am tired. Everyone's tired of my turmoil.

## Alfred Corning Clark
  (1916–1961)

You read the *New York Times*
every day at recess,
but in its dry
obituary, a list
of your wives, nothing is news,
except the ninety-five
thousand dollar engagement ring
you gave the sixth.
Poor rich boy,
you were unseasonably adult
at taking your time,
and died at forty-five.
Poor Al Clark,
behind your enlarged,
hardly recognizable photograph,
I feel the pain.
You were alive. You are dead.
You wore bow-ties and dark
blue coats, and sucked
wintergreen or cinnamon lifesavers
to sweeten your breath.
There must be something –
some one to praise
your triumphant diffidence,
your refusal of exertion,
the intelligence
that pulsed in the sensitive,
pale concavities of your forehead.
You never worked,
and were third in the form.
I owe you something –
I was befogged,

and you were too bored,
quick and cool to laugh.
You are dear to me, Alfred;
our reluctant souls united
in our unconventional
illegal games of chess
on the St. Mark's quadrangle.
You usually won –
motionless
as a lizard in the sun.

# July in Washington

The stiff spokes of this wheel
touch the sore spots of the earth.

On the Potomac, swan-white
power launches keep breasting the sulphurous wave.

Otters slide and dive and slick back their hair,
raccoons clean their meat in the creek.

On the circles, green statues ride like South American
liberators above the breeding vegetation –

prongs and spearheads of some equatorial
backland that will inherit the globe.

The elect, the elected . . . they come here bright as dimes,
and die disheveled and soft.

We cannot name their names, or number their dates -
circle on circle, like rings on a tree –

but we wish the river had another shore,
some farther range of delectable mountains,

distant hills powdered blue as a girl's eyelid.
It seems the least little shove would land us there,

that only the slightest repugnance of our bodies
we no longer control could drag us back.

# Buenos Aires

In my room at the Hotel Continentál
a thousand miles from nowhere,
I heard
the bulky, beefy breathing of the herds.

Cattle furnished my new clothes:
my coat of limp, chestnut-colored suede,
my sharp shoes
that hurt my toes.

A false fin de siècle decorum
snored over Buenos Aires
lost in the pampas
and run by the barracks.

All day I read about newspaper coups d'état
of the leaden, internecine generals –
lumps of dough on the chessboard – and never saw
their countermarching tanks.

Along the sunlit cypress walks
of the Republican martyrs' graveyard,
hundreds of one-room Roman temples
hugged their neo-classical catafalques.

Literal commemorative busts
preserved the frogged coats
and fussy, furrowed foreheads
of those soldier bureaucrats.

By their brazen doors
a hundred marble goddesses
wept like willows. I found rest
by cupping a soft palm to each hard breast.

I was the worse for wear,
and my breath whitened the winter air
next morning, when Buenos Aires filled
with frowning, starch-collared crowds.

## Soft Wood

*for Harriet Winslow*

Sometimes I have supposed seals
must live as long as the Scholar Gypsy.
Even in their barred pond at the zoo they are happy,
and no sunflower turns
more delicately to the sun
without a wincing of the will.

Here too in Maine things bend to the wind forever.
After two years away, one must get used
to the painted soft wood staying bright and clean,
to the air blasting an all-white wall whiter,
as it blows through curtain and screen
touched with salt and evergreen.

The green juniper berry spills crystal-clear gin,
and even the hot water in the bathtub
is more than water,
and rich with the scouring effervescence
of something healing,
the illimitable salt.

Things last, but sometimes for days here
only children seem fit to handle children,
and there is no utility or inspiration
in the wind smashing without direction.
The fresh paint
on the captains' houses hides softer wood.

Their square-riggers used to whiten
the four corners of the globe,
but it's no consolation to know
the possessors seldom outlast the possessions,
once warped and mothered by their touch.
Shed skin will never fit another wearer.

Yet the seal pack will bark past my window
summer after summer.
This is the season
when our friends may and will die daily.
Surely the lives of the old
are briefer than the young.

Harriet Winslow, who owned this house,
was more to me than my mother.
I think of you far off in Washington,
breathing in the heat wave
and air-conditioning, knowing
each drug that numbs alerts another nerve to pain.

# For the Union Dead

*'Relinquunt Omnia Servare Rem Publicam.'*

The old South Boston Aquarium stands
in a Sahara of snow now. Its broken windows are boarded.
The bronze weathervane cod has lost half its scales.
The airy tanks are dry.

Once my nose crawled like a snail on the glass;
my hand tingled
to burst the bubbles
drifting from the noses of the cowed, compliant fish.

My hand draws back. I often sigh still
for the dark downward and vegetating kingdom
of the fish and reptile. One morning last March,
I pressed against the new barbed and galvanized

fence on the Boston Common. Behind their cage,
yellow dinosaur steamshovels were grunting
as they cropped up tons of mush and grass
to gouge their underworld garage.

Parking spaces luxuriate like civic
sandpiles in the heart of Boston.
A girdle of orange, Puritan-pumpkin colored girders
braces the tingling Statehouse,

shaking over the excavations, as it faces Colonel Shaw
and his bell-cheeked Negro infantry
on St. Gaudens' shaking Civil War relief,
propped by a plank splint against the garage's earthquake.

Two months after marching through Boston,
half the regiment was dead;
at the dedication,
William James could almost hear the bronze Negroes
    breathe.

Their monument sticks like a fishbone
in the city's throat.
Its Colonel is as lean
as a compass-needle.

He has an angry wrenlike vigilance,
a greyhound's gentle tautness;
he seems to wince at pleasure,
and suffocate for privacy.

He is out of bounds now. He rejoices in man's lovely,
peculiar power to choose life and die –
when he leads his black soldiers to death,
he cannot bend his back.

On a thousand small town New England greens,
the old white churches hold their air
of sparse, sincere rebellion; frayed flags
quilt the graveyards of the Grand Army of the Republic.

The stone statues of the abstract Union Soldier
grow slimmer and younger each year –
wasp-waisted, they doze over muskets
and muse through their sideburns . . .

Shaw's father wanted no monument
except the ditch,
where his son's body was thrown
and lost with his 'niggers'.

The ditch is nearer.
There are no statues for the last war here;
on Boylston Street, a commercial photograph
shows Hiroshima boiling

over a Mosler Safe, the 'Rock of Ages'
that survived the blast. Space is nearer.
When I crouch to my television set,
the drained faces of Negro school-children rise like balloons.

Colonel Shaw
is riding on his bubble,
he waits
for the blessèd break.

The Aquarium is gone. Everywhere,
giant finned cars nose forward like fish;
a savage servility
slides by on grease.

# Waking Early Sunday Morning

O to break loose, like the chinook
salmon jumping and falling back,
nosing up to the impossible
stone and bone-crushing waterfall –
raw-jawed, weak-fleshed there, stopped by ten
steps of the roaring ladder, and then
to clear the top on the last try,
alive enough to spawn and die.

Stop, back off. The salmon breaks
water, and now my body wakes
to feel the unpolluted joy
and criminal leisure of a boy –
no rainbow smashing a dry fly
in the white run is free as I,
here squatting like a dragon on
time's hoard before the day's begun!

Vermin run for their unstopped holes;
in some dark nook a fieldmouse rolls
a marble, hours on end, then stops;
the termite in the woodwork sleeps –
listen, the creatures of the night
obsessive, casual, sure of foot,
go on grinding, while the sun's
daily remorseful blackout dawns.

Fierce, fireless mind, running downhill.
Look up and see the harbor fill:
business as usual in eclipse
goes down to the sea in ships –
wake of refuse, dacron rope,
bound for Bermuda or Good Hope,

all bright before the morning watch
the wine-dark hulls of yawl and ketch.

I watch a glass of water wet
with a fine fuzz of icy sweat,
silvery colors touched with sky,
serene in their neutrality –
yet if I shift, or change my mood,
I see some object made of wood,
background behind it of brown grain,
to darken it, but not to stain.

O that the spirit could remain
tinged but untarnished by its strain!
Better dressed and stacking birch,
or lost with the Faithful at Church –
anywhere, but somewhere else!
And now the new electric bells,
clearly chiming, 'Faith of our fathers,'
and now the congregation gathers.

O Bible chopped and crucified
in hymns we hear but do not read,
none of the milder subtleties
of grace or art will sweeten these
stiff quatrains shovelled out four-square –
they sing of peace, and preach despair;
yet they gave darkness some control,
and left a loophole for the soul.

No, put old clothes on, and explore
the corners of the woodshed for
its dregs and dreck: tools with no handle,
ten candle-ends not worth a candle,
old lumber banished from the Temple,
damned by Paul's precept and example,
cast from the kingdom, banned in Israel,
the wordless sign, the tinkling cymbal.

When will we see Him face to face?
Each day, He shines through darker glass.
In this small town where everything
is known, I see His vanishing
emblems, His white spire and flag-
pole sticking out above the fog,
like old white china doorknobs, sad,
slight, useless things to calm the mad.

Hammering military splendor,
top-heavy Goliath in full armor –
little redemption in the mass
liquidations of their brass,
elephant and phalanx moving
with the times and still improving,
when that kingdom hit the crash:
a million foreskins stacked like trash . . .

Sing softer! But what if a new
diminuendo brings no true
tenderness, only restlessness,
excess, the hunger for success,
sanity of self-deception
fixed and kicked by reckless caution,
while we listen to the bells –
anywhere, but somewhere else!

O to break loose. All life's grandeur
is something with a girl in summer . . .
elated as the President
girdled by his establishment
this Sunday morning, free to chaff
his own thoughts with his bear-cuffed staff,
swimming nude, unbuttoned, sick
of his ghost-written rhetoric!

No weekends for the gods now. Wars
flicker, earth licks its open sores,

fresh breakage, fresh promotions, chance
assassinations, no advance.
Only man thinning out his kind
sounds through the Sabbath noon, the blind
swipe of the pruner and his knife
busy about the tree of life . . .

Pity the planet, all joy gone
from this sweet volcanic cone;
peace to our children when they fall
in small war on the heels of small
war — until the end of time
to police the earth, a ghost
orbiting forever lost
in our monotonous sublime.

# Near the Ocean
### for E. H. L.

The house is filled. The last heartthrob
thrills through her flesh. The hero stands,
stunned by the applauding hands,
and lifts her head to please the mob . . .
No, young and starry-eyed, the brother
and sister wait before their mother,
old iron-bruises, powder, 'Child,
these breasts . . .' He knows. And if she's killed

his treadmill heart will never rest –
his wet mouth pressed to some slack breast,
or shifting over on his back . . .
The severed radiance filters back,
athirst for nightlife – gorgon head,
fished up from the Aegean dead,
with all its stranded snakes uncoiled,
here beheaded and despoiled.

We hear the ocean. Older seas
and deserts give asylum, peace
to each abortion and mistake.
Lost in the Near Eastern dreck,
the tyrant and tyrannicide
lie like the bridegroom and the bride;
the battering ram, abandoned, prone,
beside the apeman's phallic stone.

Betrayals! Was it the first night?
They stood against a black and white
inland New England backdrop. No dogs
there, horse or hunter, only frogs
chirring from the dark trees and swamps.
Elms watching like extinguished lamps.

Knee-high hedges of black sheep
encircling them at every step.

Some subway-green coldwater flat,
its walls tattooed with neon light,
then high delirious squalor, food
burned down with vodka . . . menstrual blood
caking the covers, when they woke
to the dry, childless Sunday walk,
saw cars on Brooklyn Bridge descend
through steel and coal dust to land's end.

Was it years later when they met,
and summer's coarse last-quarter drought
had dried the hardveined elms to bark –
lying like people out of work,
dead sober, cured, recovered, on
the downslope of some gritty green,
all access barred with broken glass;
and dehydration browned the grass?

Is it this shore? Their eyes worn white
as moons from hitting bottom? Night,
the sandfleas scissoring their feet,
the sandbed cooling to concrete,
one borrowed blanket, lights of cars
shining down at them like stars? . . .
Sand built the lost Atlantis . . . sand,
Atlantic ocean, condoms, sand.

Sleep, sleep. The ocean, grinding stones,
can only speak the present tense;
nothing will age, nothing will last,
or take corruption from the past.
A hand, your hand then! I'm afraid
to touch the crisp hair on your head –
Monster loved for what you are,
till time, that buries us, lay bare.

# The Ruins of Time

(Quevedo, *Miré los muros de la patria mía* and
*Buscas en Roma a Roma, ¡O peregrino!*)

I

I saw the musty shingles of my house,
raw wood and fixed once, now a wash of moss
eroded by the ruin of the age
turning all fair and green things into waste.
I climbed the pasture. I saw the dim sun drink
the ice just thawing from the bouldered fallow,
woods crowd the foothills, seize last summer's field,
and higher up, the sickly cattle bellow.
I went into my house. I saw how dust
and ravel had devoured its furnishing;
even my cane was withered and more bent,
even my sword was coffined up in rust –
there was no hilt left for the hand to try.
Everything ached, and told me I must die.

II

You search in Rome for Rome? O Traveller!
in Rome itself, there is no room for Rome,
the Aventine is its own mound and tomb,
only a corpse receives the worshipper.
And where the Capitol once crowned the forum,
are medals ruined by the hands of time;
they show how more was lost to chance and time
than Hannibal or Caesar could consume.
The Tiber flows still, but its waste laments
a city that has fallen in its grave –
each wave's a woman beating at her breast.
O Rome! From all your palms, dominion, bronze
and beauty, what was firm has fled. What once
was fugitive maintains its permanence.

48

# Dawn

The building's color is penny-postcard pale
as new wood – thirty stories, or a hundred?
The distant view-windows glisten like little cells;
on a wafer balcony, too thin to sit on,
a crimson blazer hangs, a replica
of my own from Harvard – hollow, blowing,
shining its Harvard shield to the fall air. . . .
Eve and Adam, adventuring from the ache
of the first sleep, met forms less primitive
and functional, when they gazed on the stone-ax
and Hawaiian fig-leaf hanging from their fig-tree. . . .
Nothing more established, pure and lonely,
than the early Sunday morning in New York –
the sun on high burning, and most cars dead.

## Walks

In those days no *casus belli* to fight the earth
for the familial, hidden fundamental –
on their walks they scoured the hills to find a girl,
tomorrow promised the courage to die content.
The willow stump put out thin wands in leaf,
green, fleeting flashes of unmerited joy;
the first garden, each morning . . . the first man –
birds laughing at us from the distant trees,
troubadours of laissez-faire and love.
Conservatives only want to have the earth,
the great beast clanking its chain of vertebrae. . . .
Am I a free man, if I have no servant?
If at the end of the long walk, my old dog dies of joy
when I sit down, a poor man at my fire?

## Orestes' Dream

'As I sleep, our saga comes out clarified:
why for three weeks mother toured the countryside,
buying up earthenware, big pots and urns,
barbarous potsherds, such as the thirsty first
archaeologists broke on their first digs . . . not *our* art –
kingly the clay, common the workmanship.
For three weeks mother's lover kept carving
chess-sets, green leaf, red leaf, as tall as urns,
modern Viking design for tribal Argos. . . .
When Agamemnon, my father, came home at last,
he was skewered and held bubbling like an ox,
his eyes crossed in the great strain of the heat –
my mother danced with a wicker bullshead by his urn.
Can I call the police against my own family?'

## Marcus Cato 234–149 BC

My live telephone swings crippled to solitude
two feet from my ear; as so often and so often,
I hold your dialogue away to breathe –
still this is love, Old Cato forgoing his wife,
then jumping her in thunderstorms like *Juppiter Tonans*;
his forthrightness gave him long days of solitude,
then deafness changed his gifts for rule to genius.
Cato knew from the Greeks that empire is hurry,
and dominion never goes to the phlegmatic –
it was hard to be Demosthenes in his stone-deaf Senate:
'Carthage must die,' he roared . . . and Carthage died.
He knew a blindman looking for gold
in a heap of dust must take the dust with the gold,
Rome, if built at all, must be built in a day.

# Dante 4. Paolo and Francesca

And she to me, 'What sorrow is greater to us
than returning from misery to the sweet time?
If you will know the first root of our love,
I'll speak as one who must both speak and weep.
On that day we were reading for dalliance
of Lancelot, and how love brought him down;
we were alone there and without suspicion,
often something we read made our eyes meet –
we lost color. A single moment destroyed us: reading
how her loved smile was kissed by such a lover.
He who never will be divided from me
came to me trembling, and kissed my shaking mouth.
That book and he who wrote it was a bawd,
a Galahalt. That day we read no further.'

## Cow

The moon is muffled behind a ledge of cloud,
briefly douses its bonfire on the harbor. . . .
Machiavelli despised those spuriously fought
Italian mounted-mercenary battles;
Corinthian tactics, Greek met Greek; one death,
he died of a stroke, but not the stroke of battle.
The Italians were not diehards even for peace –
our police hit more to terrorize than kill;
clubs break and minds, women hosed down stairs –
am I crippled for life? . . . A cow has guts,
screwed, she lives for it as much as we,
a three-day mother, then a working mother;
the calf goes to the calfpool. . . . When their barn has been
    burned,
cows will look into the sunset and tremble.

## Cranach's Man-Hunt

Composed, you will say, for our forever friendship,
almost one arm around our many shoulders,
a cloud darkens the stream of the photograph,
friends bound by birth and faith . . . one German outing.
We are game for the deer-hunt, aged five to ninety,
seniority no key to who will die
on this clearing of blown, coarse grass, a trap in the
    landscape,
a green bow in the bend of a choppy, lavender stream,
eighteen or nineteen of us, bounding, swimming –
stags and does . . . the Kaiser Maximilian
and the wise Saxon Elector, screened by one clump,
winch their crossbows . . . the horsemen, picadors,
whipped to action by their beautiful, verminous dogs . . .
this battle the Prince has never renounced or lost.

## Rimbaud 2. A Knowing Girl

In the cigar-brown dining room perfumed
with a smell of fruitbowls and shellac,
I was wolfing my plate of God knows what
Belgian dish. I sprawled in a huge chair,
I listened to the clock tock while I ate.
Then the kitchen door opened with a bang,
the housemaid came in . . . who knows why . . . her blouse
half-open and her hair wickedly set. She passed
her little finger trembling across her cheek,
pink and white peach bloom, and made a grimace
with her childish mouth, and coming near me
tidied my plates to make me free . . .
then – just like that, to get a kiss of course –
whispered, 'Feel this, my cheek has caught a cold.'

# Little Millionaire's Pad, Chicago

The little millionaire's is a sheen of copies;
at first glance most everything is French;
a sonata scored *sans rigueur*
is on a muddy-white baby grand piano,
the little plaster bust on it, small as a medallion,
is Franz Schubert below the colored blow-up
of the master's wife, executive Bronzino –
his frantic touch to antique her! Out the window,
two cunning cylinder apartment towers –
below the apartments, six spirals of car garage,
below the cars, yachts at moorings – more Louis Quinze
and right than anything of the millionaire's,
except the small daughter's bedroom, perfect with posters:
'Do not enter. Sock it to me, Baby.'

## To Daddy

I think, though I didn't believe it, you were my airhole,
and resigned perhaps from the Navy to be an airhole –
that Mother not warn me to put my socks on before my
    shoes.

## Will Not Come Back

*(Volveran)*

Dark swallows will doubtless come back killing
the injudicious nightflies with a clack of the beak;
but these that stopped full flight to see your beauty
and my good fortune . . . as if they knew our names –
they'll not come back. The thick lemony honeysuckle,
climbing from the earthroot to your window,
will open more beautiful blossoms to the evening;
but these . . . like dewdrops, trembling, shining, falling,
the tears of day – they'll not come back. . . .
Some other love will sound his fireword for you
and wake your heart, perhaps, from its cool sleep;
but silent, absorbed, and on his knees,
as men adore God at the altar, as I love you –
don't blind yourself, you'll not be loved like that.

## Picture in *The Literary Life, a Scrapbook*

A mag. photo, before I was I, or my books –
a listener. . . . A cheekbone gumballs out my cheek;
too much live hair. My wife caught in that eye blazes,
an egg would boil in the tension of that hand,
my untied shoestrings write my name in the dust. . . .
I lean against the tree, and sharpen bromides
to serve our great taskmaster, the New Critic,
who loved the writing better than we ourselves. . . .
In those days, if I pressed an ear to the earth,
I heard the bass growl of Hiroshima.
In the *Scrapbook*, it's only the old die classics:
one foot in the grave, two fingers in their Life.
Who would rather be his indexed correspondents
than the boy Keats spitting out blood for time to breathe?

## Robert Frost

Robert Frost at midnight, the audience gone
to vapor, the great act laid on the shelf in mothballs,
his voice is musical and raw – he writes in the flyleaf:
*For Robert from Robert, his friend in the art.*
'Sometimes I feel too full of myself,' I say.
And he, misunderstanding, 'When I am low,
I stray away. My son wasn't your kind. The night
we told him Merrill Moore would come to treat him,
he said, "I'll kill him first." One of my daughters thought
    things,
thought every male she met was out to make her;
the way she dressed, she couldn't make a whorehouse.'
And I, 'Sometimes I'm so happy I can't stand myself.'
And he, 'When I am too full of joy, I think
how little good my health did anyone near me.'

## Caracas 1

Through another of our cities without a center,
Los Angeles, and with as many cars
per foot, and past the 20-foot neon sign
for *Coppertone* on the cathedral, past the envied,
$700 per capita a year
in jerry skyscraper living slabs – to the White House
of El Presidente Leoni, his small men with 18-
inch repeating pistols, firing 45 bullets a minute,
two armed guards frozen beside us, and our champagne . . .
someone bugging the President: 'Where are the girls?'
And the enclosed leader, quite a fellow, saying,
'I don't know where yours are, I know where to find
     mine'. . . .
This house, this pioneer democracy, built
on foundations, not of rock, but blood as hard as rock.

## The Restoration

The old king enters his study with the police;
it's much like mine left in my hands a month:
unopened letters, the thousand dead cigarettes,
open books, yogurt cups in the unmade bed –
the old king enters his study with the police,
but all in all his study is much worse than mine;
an edge of malice shows the thumb of man:
frames smashed, their honorary honours lost,
all his unopened letters have been answered.
He halts at woman-things that can't be his,
and says, 'To think that human beings did this!'
The sergeant picks up a defiled *White Goddess*,
or the old king's offprints on ideograms,
'Would a human beings do this things to these book?'

## For Eugene McCarthy
*(July, 1968)*

I love you so. . . . Gone? Who will swear you wouldn't
have done good to the country, that fulfilment wouldn't
have done good to you – the father, as Freud says:
you? We've so little faith that anyone
ever makes anything better . . . the same and less –
ambition only makes the ambitious great.
The state lifts us, we cannot raise the state. . . . All
was yours though, lining down the balls for hours,
freedom of the hollow bowling-alley,
the thundered strikes, the boys. . . . Picking a quarrel
with you is like picking the petals of the daisy –
the game, the passing crowds, the rapid young
still brand your hand with sunflecks . . . coldly willing
to smash the ball past those who bought the park.

## Eating Out Alone

The loneliness inside me is a place,
Harvard where no one might always be someone.
When we're alone people we run from change
to the mysterious and beautiful –
I am eating alone at a small white table,
visible, ignored . . . the moment that tries the soul,
an explorer going blind in polar whiteness.
Yet everyone who is seated is a lay,
or Paul Claudel, at the next table declaiming:
'*L'Académie Groton, eh, c'est une école de cochons.*'
He soars from murdered English to killing French,
no word unheard, no sentence understood –
a vocabulary to mortify Racine . . .
the minotaur steaming in a maze of eloquence.

## Killer Whale Tank

Even their immensity feels the hand of man. . . .
Forming himself in an S-curve before her,
swimming side by side and belly to belly
inches distant, each one stroking the other,
feather touch of a flipper across her belly;
he teases, nuzzles and lightly bites her nose,
and with a fluke titillates the vulva –
he awakes a woman. . . . With her closed mouth she rubs
his genital slit afire, and scoots away
a fraction of a second before explosion;
then, runs straight to him and will not turn aside,
seeking the common sleep that hands them back to life.
Whales meet in love and part in friendship – swoosh. . . .
The Killer's sorrow is he has no hands.

## Verlaine, Etc.

The tender Falstaffian ugh of Verlaine,
*I who have no mind have more than you. . . .*
*Are only drunken words cold sober true?*
Paul Valéry's assault on modesty,
*To be understood is the worst disaster.*
Aside from money, literary success
was small compensation for their vanity:
to be condemned by people who never read them,
to have been useful to poets devoid of talent.
Do we like Auden want a hundred mute admirers,
or the daily surf of spit and fanmail from all
the known shores tiding in and out? . . .
The muse is a loser, she is sort of sad dirty –
publication might just scour her clean.

## Last Things, Black Pines at 4 a.m.

Imperfect enough once for all at thirty,
in his last days Van Gogh painted as if
he were hurling everything he had: clothes,
bed and furniture against the door
to keep out a robber – he would have roughened
my black pines imperceptibly withdrawing
from the blue back cold of morning sky,
black pines disengaging from blue ice –
for imperfection is the language of art.
Even the best writer in his best lines
is incurably imperfect, crying for truth, knowledge,
honesty, inspiration he cannot have –
after a show of effort, Valéry
and Trollope the huntsman are happy to drop out.

# For Elizabeth Bishop 4

The new painting must live on iron rations,
rushed brushstrokes, indestructible paint-mix,
fluorescent lofts instead of French *plein air*.
Albert Ryder let his crackled amber moonscapes
ripen in sunlight. His painting was repainting,
his tiniest work weighs heavy in the hand.
Who is killed if the horseman never cry halt?
Have you seen an inchworm crawl on a leaf,
cling to the very end, revolve in air,
feeling for something to reach to something? Do
you still hang your words in air, ten years
unfinished, glued to your notice board, with gaps
or empties for the unimaginable phrase –
unerring Muse who makes the casual perfect?

## Women, Children, Babies, Cows, Cats

'It was at My Lai or Sonmy or something,
it was this afternoon. . . . We had these orders,
we had all night to think about it –
we was to burn and kill, then there'd be nothing
standing, women, children, babies, cows, cats. . . .
As soon as we hopped the choppers, we started shooting.
I remember . . . as we was coming up upon one area
in Pinkville, a man with a gun . . . running – this lady . . .
Lieutenant LaGuerre said, "Shoot her." I said,
"You shoot her, I don't want to shoot no lady."
She had one foot in the door. . . . When I turned her,
there was this little one-month-year-old baby
I thought was her gun. It kind of cracked me up.'

## Identification in Belfast

*(I.R.A. Bombing)*

The British Army now carries two rifles,
one with rubber rabbit-pellets for children,
the other's of course for the Provisionals. . . .
'When they first showed me the boy, I thought oh good,
it's not him because he is a blonde –
I imagine his hair was singed dark by the bomb.
He had nothing on him to identify him,
except this box of joke trick matches;
he liked to have them on him, even at mass.
The police were unhurried and wonderful,
they let me go on trying to strike a match . . .
I just wouldn't stop – you cling to anything –
I couldn't believe I couldn't light one match –
only joke-matches. . . . Then I knew he was Richard.'

## Last Night

Is dying harder than being already dead?
I came to my first class without a textbook,
saw the watch I mailed my daughter didn't run;
I opened an old closet door, and found myself
covered with quicklime, my face deliquescent . . .
by oversight still recognizable.
Thank God, I was the first to find myself.
Ah the swift vanishing of my older
generation – the deaths, suicide, madness
of Roethke, Berryman, Jarrell and Lowell,
'the last the most discouraging of all
surviving to dissipate *Lord Weary's Castle*
and nine subsequent useful poems
in the seedy grandiloquence of *Notebook*.'

## New Year's 1968

These conquered kings pass angrily away;
the gods die flesh and spirit and last in print,
each library is some injured tyrant's home.
This year runs out in the movies, it must be written
in bad, straightforward, unscanning sentences –
mine were downtrodden, branded on back of carbons,
lines, words, letters nailed to letters, words, lines;
the typescript looked like a Rosetta Stone.
A year's black pages. Its hero *hero demens*
immovably holding off-channel for his wreck –
ill-starred of men and crossed by their fixed stars.
The slush-ice on the east water of the Hudson
rose-heather this New Year sunset; the open channel,
bright sky, bright sky, a carbon scarred with ciphers.

# The Charles River

### 1

The sycamores throw shadows on the Charles,
as the fagged insect splinters, drops and joins
the infinite that scatters loosening leaves,
the long-haired escort and his short-skirted girl.
The black stream curves as if it led a lover –
my blood is pounding; in workaday times,
I take cold comfort from its heartelation,
its endless handstand round the single I,
the pumping and thumping of my overfevered wish. . . .
For a week my heart has pointed elsewhere:
it brings us here tonight, and ties our hands –
if we leaned forward, and should dip a finger
into the river's momentary black flow,
infinite small stars would break like fish.

### 2

The circuit of snow-topped rural roads, eight miles
to ten, might easily have been the world's top,
the North Pole, when I trailed on spreading skis
my guide, his unerring legs ten inches thick in wool,
and pinched my earlobes lest they turn to snowdrops –
hard knocks that school a lifetime; yet I went on swiping
small things. That knife, yellow-snow with eleven blades,
where is it? Somewhere, where it will outlast me,
though flawed already when I picked it up. . . .
And now, the big town river, once straight and dead as its
    highway,
shrinks to country river, bankscrub, dry ice,
a live muskrat muddying the moonlight. You trail me,
Woman, so small, if one could trust appearance,
I might be in trouble with the law.

3

No stars, only cars, the stars of man,
mount sky and highway; life is wild: ice straw
puts teeth in the shallows, the water smells and lives.
We walk a tightrope, this embankment, jewed –
no, yankeed – by highways down to a stubbly lip. . . .
Once – you weren't born then – an iron railing,
cheerless and dignified, policed this walk;
it matched the times, and had an esplanade,
stamping down grass and growth with square stone shoes;
a groan went up when the iron railing crashed. . . .
The Charles, half ink, half liquid coaldust,
bears witness to the health of industry –
wrong times, an evil dispensation; but who
can hope to enter heaven with clean hands?


4

Seen by no visible eye, our night unbroken –
our motel bedroom is putty-gray and cold,
the shivering winds thrust through its concrete cube.
A car or two, then none; since midnight none.
Highways on three levels parallel the river,
roads patrol the river in her losing struggle,
a force of nature trying to breathe beneath
a jacket of lava. We lie parallel,
parallel to the river, parallel
to six roads – unhappy and awake,
awake and naked, like a line of Greeks,
facing a second line of Greeks – like them,
willing to enter the battle, and not come out . . .
morning's breathing traffic . . . its unbroken snore.

# Mexico

## 1

The difficulties, the impossibilities . . .
I, fifty, humbled with the years' gold garbage,
dead laurel grizzling my back like spines of hay;
you, some sweet, uncertain age, say twenty-seven,
untempted, unseared by honors or deception.
What help then? Not the sun, the scarlet blossom,
and the high fever of this seventh day,
the predestined diarrhea of the pilgrim,
the multiple mosquito spots, round as pesos.
Hope not for God here, or even for the gods;
the Aztecs knew the sun, the source of life,
will die, unless we feed it human blood –
we two are clocks, and only count in time . . .
the hand a knife-edge pressed against the future.

## 3

The lizard rusty as a leaf rubbed rough
does nothing for days but puff his throat
on oxygen, and tongue up passing flies,
loves only identical rusty lizards panting:
harems worthy this lord of the universe –
each thing he does generic, and not the best.
We sit on a cliff like curs, chins pressed to thumbs –
how fragrantly our cold hands warm to the live coal!
The Toltec temples pass to dust in the dusk –
the clock dial of the rising moon, dust out of time –
two clocks set back to Montezuma's utopia . . .
as if we still wished to pull teeth with firetongs –
when they took a city, they murdered everything,
till the Spaniards, by reflex, finished them.

4

South of Boston, south of Washington,
south of any bearing . . . I walk the glazed moonlight:
dew on the grass and nobody about,
drawn on by my unlimited desire,
like a bull with a ring in his nose, a chain in the ring. . . .
We moved far, bull and cow, could one imagine
cattle obliviously pairing six long days:
up road and down, then up again passing the same
brick garden wall, stiff spines of hay stuck in my hide;
and always in full sight of everyone,
from the full sun to silhouetting sunset,
pinned by undimming lights of hurried cars. . . .
You're gone; I am learning to live in history.
What is history? What you cannot touch.


8

Three pillows, end on end, rolled in a daybed
blanket – elastic, round, untroubled. For a second,
by some hallucination of my hand
I imagined I was unwrapping you. . . .
Two immovable nuns, out of habit, too fat to leave
the dormitory, have lived ten days on tea,
bouillon cubes and cookies brought from Boston.
You curl in your metal bunk-bed like my child,
I sprawl on an elbow troubled by the floor –
nuns packing, nuns ringing the circular iron stair,
nuns in pajamas scalloped through their wrappers,
nuns boiling bouillon, tea or cookies, nuns
brewing and blanketing reproval . . .
the soul groans and laughs at its lack of stature.

# Circles

2 DAS EWIG WEIBLICHE

Birds have a finer body and tinier brain –
who asks the swallows to do drudgery,
clean, cook, pick up a peck of dust per diem?
If we knock on their homes, they wince uptight with fear,
farting about all morning past their young,
small as wasps fuming in their ash-leaf ball.
Nature lives off the life that comes to hand -
if we could feel and softly touch their being,
wasp, bee and swallow might live with us like cats.
The boiling yellow-jacket in her sack
of felon-stripe cut short above the knee
sings home . . . nerve-wrung creatures, wasp, bee and bird,
guerillas by day then keepers of the cell,
my wife in her wooden crib of seed and feed. . . .

3 OUR TWENTIETH WEDDING ANNIVERSARY 1
    (*Elizabeth*)

Leaves espaliered jade on our barn's loft window,
sky stretched on a two-pane sash . . . it doesn't open:
stab of roofdrip, this leaf, that leaf twings,
an assault the heartless leaf rejects.
The picture is too perfect for our lives:
in Chardin's stills, the paint bleeds, juice is moving.
We have weathered the wet of twenty years.
Many cripples have won their place in the race;
Emmanuel Kant remained unmarried and sane,
no one could Byronize his walk to class.
Often the player outdistances the game. . . .
This week is our first this summer to go unfretted;
we smell as green as the weeds that bruise the flower –
a house eats up the wood that made it.

## 6 THE HARD WAY

### (*Harriet*)

Don't hate your parents, or your children will hire
unknown men to bury you at your own cost.
Child, forty years younger, will we live to see
your destiny written by our hands rewritten,
your adolescence snap the feathered barb,
the phosphorescence of your wake?
Under the stars, one sleeps, is free from household,
tufts of grass and dust and tufts of grass –
night oriented to the star of youth.
I only learn from error; till lately I trusted
in the practice of my hand. In backward Maine,
ice goes in season to the tropical,
then the mash freezes back to ice, and then
the ice is broken by another wave.


## 7 WORDS FOR MUFFIN, A GUINEA-PIG

'Of late they leave the light on in my entry,
so I won't scare, though I never scare in the dark;
I bless this arrow that flies from wall to window . . .
five years and a nightlight given me to breathe –
Heidegger said spare time is ecstasy. . . .
I am not scared, although my life was short;
my sickly breathing sounded like dry leather.
*Mrs Muffin*! It clicks. I had my day.
You'll paint me like Cromwell with all my warts:
small mop with a tumor and eyes too popped for thought.
I was a rhinoceros when jumped by my sons.
I ate and bred, and then I only ate,
my life zenithed in the Lyndon Johnson 'sixties . . .
this short pound God threw on the scales, found wanting.'

# Late Summer

### 1 END OF CAMP ALAMOOSOOK
### (*Harriet*)

Less than a score, the dregs of the last day,
counselors and campers squat waiting for the ferry –
the unexpected, the exotic, the early
morning sunlight is more like premature twilight:
last day of the day, foreclosure of the camp.
Glare on the amber squatters, fire of fool's-gold –
like bits of colored glass, they cannot burn.
The Acadians must have gathered in such arcs;
a Winslow, our cousin, shipped them from Nova Scotia –
no malice, merely pushing his line of work,
herding guerillas in some Morality.
The campers suspect us, and harden in their shyness,
their gruff, faint voices hardly say hello,
singing, 'Do we love it? *We love it.*'

### 3 BRINGING A TURTLE HOME

On the road to Bangor, we spotted a domed stone,
a painted turtle petrified by fear.
I picked it up. The turtle had come a long walk,
200 millennia understudy to dinosaurs,
then their survivor. A god for the out-of-power. . . .
Faster gods come to Castine, flush yachtsmen who see
hell as a city very much like New York,
these gods give a bad past and worse future to men
who never bother to set a spinnaker;
culture without cash isn't worth their spit.
The laughter on Mount Olympus was always breezy. . . .
*Goodnight, little Boy, little Soldier, live,*
*a toy to your friend, a stone of stumbling to God –*
*sandpaper Turtle, scratching your pail for water.*

## 4 RETURNING TURTLE

Weeks hitting the road, one fasting in the bathtub,
raw hamburger mossing in the watery stoppage,
the room drenched with musk like kerosene –
no one shaved, and only the turtle washed.
He was so beautiful when we flipped him over:
greens, reds, yellows, fringe of the faded savage,
the last Sioux, old and worn, saying with weariness,
'Why doesn't the Great White Father put his red
children on wheels, and move us as he will?'
We drove to the Orland River, and watched the turtle
rush for water like rushing into marriage,
swimming in uncontaminated joy,
lovely the flies that fed that sleazy surface,
a turtle looking back at us, and blinking.

## 11 NO HEARING 4

Discovering, discovering trees light up green at night,
braking headlights-down, ransacking the roadsides
for someone strolling, fleeing to her wide goal;
passing blanks, the white Unitarian Church,
my barn on its bulwark, two daytime padlocked shacks,
the town pool drained, the old lighthouse unplugged –
I watch the muddy breakers bleach to beerfroth,
our steamer, THE STATE OF MAINE, an iceberg at
    drydock.
Your question, my questioner? It is for you –
crouched in the gelid drip of the pine in our garden,
invisible almost when found, till I toss a white raincoat
over your sky-black, blood-trim quilted stormcoat -
you saying *I would prefer not*, like Bartleby:
small deer trembly and steel in your wet nest!

## 12 OUTLIVERS
### (Harriet and Elizabeth)

'If we could reverse the world to what it changed
a hundred years ago, or even fifty,
scrupulous drudgery, sailpower, hand-made wars;
God might give us His right to live forever
despite the eroding miracle of science. . . .'
'Was everything that much grander than it is?'
'Nothing seems admirable until it fails;
but it's only people we should miss.
The Goth, retarded epochs like crab and clam,
wept, as we do, for his dead child.' We talk
like room-mates bleeding out the night to dawn.
'I hope, of course, you both will outlive me,
but you and Harriet are perhaps like countries
not yet ripe for self-determination.'


## 13 MY HEAVENLY SHINER
### (Elizabeth)

The world atop Maine and our heads is north,
zeroes through Newfoundland to Hudson Bay:
*entremets chinois et canadiens.*
A world like ours will tumble on our heads,
my heavenly Shiner, think of it curving on?
You quiver on my finger like a small
minnow swimming in a crystal ball,
flittering radiance on my flittering finger.
The fish, the shining fish, they go in circles,
not one of them will make it to the Pole –
this isn't the point though, this is not the point;
think of it going on without a life –
in you, God knows, I've had the earthly life –
we were kind of religious, we thought in images.

## 14 IT DID

*(Elizabeth)*

Luck, we've had it; our character the public's –
and yet we will ripen, ripen, know we once
did most things better, not just physical
but moral – turning in too high for love,
living twenty-four hours in one shirt or skirt,
breathless gossip, the breathless singles' service.
We could have done much worse. I hope we did
a hundred thousand things much worse! Poor X's,
chance went this way, that way with us here:
gain counted as loss, and loss as gain: our tideluck.
It did to live with, but finally all men worsen:
drones die of stud, the saint by staying virgin . . .
old jaw only smiles to bite the feeder;
corruption serenades the wilting tissue.


## 15 SEALS

If we must live again, not us; we might
go into seals, we'd handle ourselves better:
able to dawdle, able to torpedo,
all too at home in our three elements,
ledge, water and heaven – if man could restrain his hand. . . .
We flipper the harbor, blots and patches and oilslick,
so much bluer than water, we think it sky.
Creature could face creator in this suit,
fishers of fish not men. Some other August,
the easy seal might say, 'I could not sleep
last night; suddenly I could write my name. . . .'
Then all seals, preternatural like us,
would take direction, head north – their haven
green ice in a greenland never grass.

## Obit

Our love will not come back on fortune's wheel –

in the end it gets us, though a man know what he'd have:
old cars, old money, old undebased pre-Lyndon
silver, no copper rubbing through . . . old wives;
I could live such a too long time with mine.
In the end, every hypochondriac is his own prophet.
Before the final coming to rest, comes the rest
of all transcendence in a mode of being, hushing
all becoming. I'm for and with myself in my otherness,
in the eternal return of earth's fairer children,
the lily, the rose, the sun on brick at dusk,
the loved, the lover, and their fear of life,
their unconquered flux, insensate oneness, painful 'It
    was. . . .'
After loving you so much, can I forget
you for eternity, and have no other choice?

## Fishnet

Any clear thing that blinds us with surprise,
your wandering silences and bright trouvailles,
dolphin let loose to catch the flashing fish. . . .
Poets die adolescents, their beat embalms them,
the archetypal voices sing offkey;
the old actor cannot read his friends,
and nevertheless he reads himself aloud,
genius hums the auditorium dead.
The line must terminate.
Yet my heart rises, I know I've gladdened a lifetime
knotting, undoing a fishnet of tarred rope;
the net will hang on the wall when the fish are eaten,
nailed like illegible bronze on the futureless future.

# Redcliffe Square

## 1 LIVING IN LONDON

I learn to live without ice and like the Queen;
we didn't like her buildings when they stood,
but soon Victoria's manly oak was quartered,
knickknacks dropped like spiders from the whatnot,
grandparents and their unmarried staffs decamped
for our own bobbed couples of the swimming twenties,
too giddy to destroy the homes they fled.
These houses, no two the same, tremble up six stories
to dissimilar Flemish pie-slice peaks,
shaped by constructor's pipes and scaffolding –
aboriginal like a jungle gym.
Last century's quantity brick has a sour redness
that time, I fear, does nothing to appease,
condemned by age, rebuilt by desolation.

## 2 WINDOW

Tops of the midnight trees move helter skelter
to ruin, if passion can hurt the classical
in the limited window of the easel painter –
love escapes our hands. We open the curtains:
a square of white-faced houses swerving, foaming,
the swagger of the world and chalk of London.
At each turn the houses wall the path of meeting,
and yet we meet, stand taking in the storm.
Even in provincial capitals,
storms will rarely enter a human house,
the crude and homeless wet is windowed out.
We stand and hear the pummelling unpurged,
almost uneducated by the world –
the tops of the moving trees move helter skelter.

The cattle have stopped on Godstow Meadow,
the peacock wheels his tail to move the heat,
then pivots changing to a wicker chair,
tiara of thistle on his shitty bobtail.
The feathertouch of May in England, but the heat
is American summer. Two weeks use up two months;
at home the colleges are closed for summer,
the students march, Brassman lances Cambodia –
he has lost his pen, his sword folds in his hand like felt.
Is truth here with us, if I sleep well? –
*the ten or twelve years my coeval gives himself*
*for the new bubble of his divorce . . . ten or twelve years –*
this air so estranged and hot I might be home. . . .
We have climbed above the wind to breathe.


4 OXFORD

We frittered on the long meadow of the Thames,
our shoes laminated with yellow flower –
nothing but the soft of the marsh, the moan of cows,
the rooster-peacock. Before we had arrived,
rising stars illuminated Oxford –
the Aztecs knew these stars would fail to rise
if forbidden the putrifaction of our flesh,
the victims' viscera laid out like tiles
on fishponds changed to yellow flowers,
the goldfinchnest, the phosphorous of the ocean
blowing ambergris and ambergris,
dolphin kissing dolphin with a smirking smile,
not loving one object and thinking of another.
Our senses want to please us, if we please them.

### 6 SYMPTOMS

A dog seems to lap water from the pipes,
a wheeze of dogsmell and dogcompanionship –
life-enhancing water brims my bath –
(the bag of waters or the lake of the grave . . .?)
from the palms of my feet to my wet neck –
I have no mother to lift me in her arms.
I feel my old infection, it comes once yearly:
lowered good humor, then an ominous
rise of irritable enthusiasm. . . .
Three dolphins bear our little toilet-stand,
the grin of the eyes rebukes the scowl of the lips,
they are crazy with the thirst. I soak,
examining and then examining
what I really have against myself.

### 7 DIAGNOSIS: TO CAROLINE IN SCOTLAND

The frowning morning glares by afternoon;
the gay world in purple and orange drag,
Child-Bible pictures, perishables:
oranges and red cabbage sold in carts.
The sun that lights their hearts lights mine?
I see it burn on my right hand, and see
my skin, when bent, is finely wrinkled batwing.
Since you went, our stainless steelware ages,
like the young doctor writing my prescription:
*The hospital.* My twentieth in twenty years. . . .
Seatrout run past you in the Hebrides –
the gay are psychic, centuries from now,
not a day older, they'll flutter garish colors,
salmontrout amok in Redcliffe Square.

# Hospital

## 1 SHOES

Too many go express to the house of rest,
buffooning, to-froing on the fringe of being,
one foot in life, and little right to that:
'I had to stop this business going on,
I couldn't attack my doctor anymore,
he lost his nerve for running out on life. . . .'
'Where I am not,' we chime, 'is where I am.'
Dejection washes our pollution bare.
My shoes? Did they walk out on me last night,
and streak into the glitter of the blear?
I see two dirty white, punctured tennis-shoes,
empty and planted on the one-man path.
I have no doubt where they will go. They walk
the one life offered from the many chosen.

# Hospital II

## 1 VOICES

'What a record year, even for us –
last March, I knew you'd manage by yourself,
you were the true you; now finally
your clowning makes visitors want to call a taxi,
you tease the patients as if they were your friends,
your real friends who want to save your image
from this genteel, disgraceful hospital.
Your trousers are worn to a mirror. . . . That new creature,
when I hear her name, I have to laugh.
You left two houses and two thousand books,
a workbarn by the ocean, and two slaves
to kneel and wait upon you hand and foot –
tell us why in the name of Jesus.' Why
am I clinging here so foolishly alone?

## 3 OLD SNAPSHOT FROM VENICE 1952

From the salt age, yes from the salt age,
courtesans, Christians fill the churchyard close;
that silly swelled tree is a spook with a twig for a head.
Carpaccio's Venice is as wide as the world,
Jerome and his lion lope to work unfeared. . . .
In Torcello, the stone lion I snapped behind you,
*venti anni fa*, still keeps his poodled hair –
wherever I move this snapshot, you have moved –
it's twenty years. The courtesans and lions
swim in Carpaccio's brewing tealeaf color.
Was he the first in the trade of painting to tell tales? . . .
You are making Boston in the sulfury a.m.,
dropping Harriet at camp, Old Love,
Eternity, You . . . a future told by tealeaves.

# Caroline

### 4 MARRIAGE?

'I think of you every minute of the day,
I love you every minute of the day;
you gone is *hollow, bored, unbearable.*
I feel under some emotional anaesthetic,
unable to plan or think or write or feel;
*mais ca ira*, these things will go, I feel
in an odd way against appearances,
things will come out right with us, perhaps.
As you say, we got across the Godstow Marsh,
reached Cumberland and its hairbreadth Roman roads,
climbed Hadrian's Wall, and scared the stinking Pict.
Marriage? That's another story. We saw
the diamond glare of morning on the tar.
For a minute had the road as if we owned it.'

## Summer Between Terms

### 1

The day's so calm and muggy I sweat tears,
the summer's cloudcap and the summer's heat. . . .
Surely good writers write all possible wrong –
are we so conscience-dark and cataract-blind,
we only blame in others what they blame in us?
(The sentence writes *we*, when charity wants *I*. . . .)
It takes such painful mellowing to use error. . . .
I have stood too long on a chair or ladder,
branch-lightning forking through my thought and veins –
I cannot hang my heavy picture straight.
I can't see myself . . . in the cattery,
the tomcats doze till the litters are eatable,
then find their kittens and chew off their breakable heads.
They told us by harshness to win the stars.

### 2

Plains, trains, lorries simmer through the garden,
the reviewer sent by God to humble me
ransacking my bags of dust for silver spoons –
he and I go on typing to go on living.
There are ways to live on words in England –
reading for trainfare, my host ruined on wine,
my ear gone bad from clinging to the ropes.
I'd take a lower place, eat my toad hourly;
even big frauds wince at fraudulence,
and squirm from small incisions in the self –
they live on timetable with no time to tell.
I'm sorry, I run with the hares now, not the hounds.
I waste hours writing in and writing out a line,
as if listening to conscience were telling the truth.

# Fall Weekend at *Milgate*

### 1

The day says nothing, and lacks for nothing . . . God;
but it's moonshine trying to gold-cap my life,
asking fees from the things I lived and loved,
pilgrim on this hard-edge Roman road.
Your portrait is fair-faced with your honesty,
the painter, your first husband, made girls stare.
Your wall mirror, a mat of plateglass sapphire,
mirror scrolls and claspleaves, shows this face,
huge eyes and dawn-gaze, rumination unruffled,
unlearning apparently, since 1952. . . .
I watch a feverish huddle of shivering cows;
you sit making a fishspine from a chestnut leaf.
We are at our crossroads, we are astigmatic
and stop uncomfortable, we are humanly low.

### 2

The soaking leaves, green yellow, hold like rubber,
longer than our eyes glued to the window can take;
none tumble in the inundating air. . . .
A weak eye sees miracles of birth in fall,
I'm counterclockwise . . . did we fall
last April in London, late fifties in New York?
Autumn sops on our windshield with huge green leaves;
the seasons race engines in America
burying old lumber without truce –
leaf-blight and street dye and the discard girl . . .
the lover sops gin all day to solve his puzzle.
Nature, like philosophers, has one plot,
only good for repeating what it does well:
life emerges from wood and life from life.

3

*Milgate* kept standing for four centuries,
good landlord alternating with derelict.
Most fell between. We're landlords for the weekend,
and watch October go balmy. Midday heat
draws poison from the Jacobean brick,
and invites the wilderness to our doorstep:
moles, nettles, last Sunday news, last summer's toys,
bread, cheeses, jars of honey, a felled elm
stacked like construction in the kitchen garden.
The warm day brings out wasps to share our luck,
suckers for sweets, pilots of evolution;
dozens drop in the beercans, clamber, buzz,
debating like us whether to stay and drown,
or, by losing legs and wings, take flight.

## Records

'. . . I was playing records on Sunday,
arranging all my records, and I came
on some of your voice, and started to suggest
that Harriet listen: then immediately
we both shook our heads. It was like hearing
the voice of the beloved who had died.
All this is a new feeling . . . I got the letter
this morning, the letter you wrote mc Saturday.
I thought my heart would break a thousand times,
but I would rather have read it a thousand times
than the detached unreal ones you wrote before –
you doomed to know what I have known with you,
lying with someone fighting unreality –
love vanquished by his mysterious carelessness.'

# Mermaid

### 3

Our meetings are no longer like a screening;
I see the nose on my face is just a nose,
your *bel occhi grandi* are just eyes
in the photo of you arranged as figurehead
or mermaid on the prow of a Roman dory,
bright as the morning star or a blond starlet.
Our twin black and tin Ronson butane lighters
knock on the sheet, are what they are,
too many, and burned too many cigarettes. . . .
Night darkens without your necessary call,
it's time to turn your pictures to the wall;
your moon-eyes water and your nervous throat
gruffs my directive, '*You must go now go.*'
Contralto mermaid, and stone-deaf at will.

### 5

One wondered who would see and date you next,
and grapple for the danger of your hand.
Will money drown you? Poverty, though now
in fashion, debases women as much as wealth.
You use no scent, dab brow and lash with shoeblack,
willing to face the world without more face.
I've searched the rough black ocean for you,
and saw the turbulence drop dead for you,
always lovely, even for those who had you,
Rough Slitherer in your grotto of haphazard.
I lack manhood to finish the fishing trip.
Glad to escape beguilement and the storm,
I thank the ocean that hides the fearful mermaid –
like God, I almost doubt if you exist.

# In the Mail

'Your student wrote me, if he took a plane
past Harvard, at any angle, at any height,
he'd see a person missing, *Mr Robert Lowell*.
You insist on treating Harriet as if she
were thirty or a wrestler – she is only thirteen.
She is normal and good because she had normal and good
parents. She is threatened of necessity. . . .
I love you, Darling, there's a black black void,
as black as night without you. I long to see
your face and hear your voice, and take your hand –
I'm watching a scruffy, seal-colored woodchuck graze
on weeds, then lift his greedy snout and listen;
then back to speedy feeding. He weighs a ton,
and has your familiar human aspect munching.'

# Winter and London

2 AT *OFFADO'S*

The Latin Quarter abuts on Belgravia,
three floors low as one, blocks built of blocks,
insular eighteenth century laying down
the functional with a razor in its hand,
construction too practical for conservation.
An alien should count his change here, bring a friend.
Usually on weekend nights I eat alone;
you've taken the train for *Milgate* with the children.
At *Offado's*, the staff is half the guests,
the guitar and singers wait on table,
the artist sings things unconsolable:
'Girls of Majorca. Where is my Sombrero?
Leave me alone and let me talk and love me –
a cod in garlic, a carafe of cruel rosé.'

# Before Woman

1 BEFORE THE DAWN OF WOMAN

'Gazing close-up at your underjaw,
a blazon of barbaric decoration,
a sprinkle of black rubies, clots from shaving,
panting in measure to your wearied breath,
I see the world before the dawn of woman,
a jungle of long-horned males, their scab of rapine,
rhinoceros on Eden's rhinoceros rock. . . .
You hold me in the hollow of your hand –
a man is free to play or free to slack,
shifty past the reach of ridicule.
A woman loving is serious and disarmed,
she is less distracted than a pastured mare,
munching as if life depended on munching. . . .
Like the animals, I am humorless.'

# Marriage

Leaf-lace, a simple intricate design –
if you were not inside it, nothing much,
bits of glinting silver on crinkled lace –
you fall perhaps metallic and as good.
Hard to work out the fact that makes you good,
whole spirit wrought from toys and nondescript,
though nothing less than the best woman in the world.
Cold the green shadows, iron the seldom sun,
harvest has worn her swelling shirt to dirt.
Agony says we cannot live in one house,
or under a common name. This was the sentence –
I have lost everything. I feel a strength,
I have walked five miles, and still desire to throw
my feet off, be asleep with you . . . asleep and young.

8 LETTER

'I despair of letters. You say I wrote H. isn't
interested in the thing happening to you now.
So what? A fantastic untruth, misprint, something;
I meant the London scene's no big concern, just you. . . .
She's absolutely beautiful, gay, etc.
I've a horror of turmoiling her before she flies
to Mexico, alone, brave, half Spanish-speaking.
Children her age don't sit about talking *the thing*
about their parents. I do talk about you,
and I have never denied I miss you . . .
I guess we'll make Washington this weekend;
it's a demonstration, like all demonstrations,
repetitious, gratuitous, unfresh . . . just needed.
I hope nothing is mis-said in this letter.'

## 13 ROBERT SHERIDAN LOWELL

Your midnight ambulances, the first knife-saw
of the child, feet-first, a string of tobacco tied
to your throat that won't go down, your window heaped
with brown paper bags leaking peaches and avocados,
your meals tasting like Kleenex . . . too much blood is
   seeping . . .
after twelve hours of labor to come out right,
in less than thirty seconds swimming the blood-flood:
Little Gingersnap Man, homoform,
flat and sore and alcoholic red,
only like us in owning to middle-age.
'If you touch him, he'll burn your fingers.'
'It's his health, not fever. Why are the other babies so pallid?
His navy-blue eyes tip with his head. . . . Darling,
we have escaped our death-struggle with our lives.'


## 14 OVERHANGING CLOUD

This morning the overhanging clouds are piecrust,
milelong Luxor Temples based on rich runny ooze;
my old life settles down into the archives.
It's strange having a child today, though common,
adding our further complication to
intense fragility.
Clouds go from dull to dazzle all the morning;
we have not grown as our child did in the womb,
met Satan like Milton going blind in London;
it's enough to wake without old fears,
and watch the needle-fire of the first light
bombarding off your eyelids harmlessly.
By ten the bedroom is sultry. You have double-breathed;
we are many, our bed smells of hay.

So country-alone, and O so very friendly,
our heaviness lifted from us by the night . . .
we dance out into its diamond suburbia,
and see the hill-crown's unrestricted lights –
all day these encroaching neighbors are out of sight.
Huge smudge sheep in burden becloud the grass,
they swell on moonlight and weigh two hundred pounds –
hulky as you in your white sheep-coat, as nervous to
    gallop. . . .
The Christ-Child's drifter shepherds have left this field,
gone the shepherd's breezy too predictable pipe.
Nothing's out of earshot in this daylong night;
nothing can be human without man.
What is worse than hearing the late-born child crying –
and each morning waking up glad we wake?


16 MORNING AWAY FROM YOU

This morning in oystery Colchester, a single
skeleton black rose sways on my flour-sack window –
Hokusai's hairfine assertion of dearth.
It wrings a cry of absence. . . . My host's new date,
apparently naked, carrying all her clothes
sways through the dawn in my bedroom to the shower.
Goodmorning. My nose runs, I feel for my blood,
happy you save mine and hand it on,
now death becomes an ingredient of my being –
my Mother and Father dying young and sixty
with the nervous systems of a child of six. . . .
I lie thinking myself to night internalized;
when I open the window, the black rose-leaves
return to inconstant greenness. A good morning, as often.

# Dolphin

My Dolphin, you only guide me by surprise,
forgetful as Racine, the man of craft,
drawn through his maze of iron composition
by the incomparable wandering voice of Phèdre.
When I was troubled in mind, you made for my body
caught in its hangman's-knot of sinking lines,
the glassy bowing and scraping of my will. . . .
I have sat and listened to too many
words of the collaborating muse,
and plotted perhaps too freely with my life,
not avoiding injury to others,
not avoiding injury to myself –
to ask compassion . . . this book, half fiction,
an eelnet made by man for the eel fighting –

my eyes have seen what my hand did.

# Homecoming

What was is . . . since 1930;
the boys in my old gang
are senior partners. They start up
bald like baby birds
to embrace retirement.

At the altar of surrender,
I met you
in the hour of credulity.
How your misfortune came out clearly
to us at twenty.

At the gingerbread casino,
how innocent the nights we made it
on our *Vesuvio* martinis
with no vermouth but vodka
to sweeten the dry gin –

the lash across my face
that night we adored . . .
soon every night and all,
when your sweet, amorous
repetition changed.

Fertility is not to the forward,
or beauty to the precipitous –
things gone wrong
clothe summer
with gold leaf.

Sometimes
I catch my mind
circling for you with glazed eye –
my lost love hunting
your lost face.

Summer to summer,
the poplars sere
in the glare –
it's a town for the young,
they break themselves against the surf.

No dog knows my smell.

## Departure

*(Intermissa, Venus, diu)*

'Waiting out the rain,
but what are you waiting for?
The storm can only stop
to get breath to begin again . . .
always in suspense to hit
the fugitive in flight.
Your clothes, moth-holed
with round cigarette burns,
sag the closet-pole.
Your books are rows of hollow suits;
"Who lives in them?"
we ask acidly,
and bring them down
flapping their paper wrappers.
So many secondary troubles,
the body's curative diversions;
but what does it matter,
if one is oneself, has something
past criticism to change to?
Not now as you were young . . .
Horace in his fifties held
a Ligurian girl
captive in the sleep of night,
followed her flying across the grass
of the Campus Martius, saw her lost
in the Tiber he could not hold.
Can you hear my first voice,
amused in sorrow,
dramatic in amusement . . .
catastrophies of description
knowing when to stop,
when not to stop?

It cannot be replayed;
only by exaggeration
could I tell the truth.
For me, neither boy
nor woman was a help.
Caught in the augmenting storm,
choice itself is wrong,
nothing said or not said tells –
a shapeless splatter of grounded rain . . .
Why, Love, why, are a few tears
scattered on my cheeks?'

## Jean Stafford, a Letter

*Towmahss Mahnn:* that's how you said it . . .
'That's how Mann must say it,' I thought.

I can go on imagining you
in your Heidelberry braids and Bavarian
peasant aprons you wore three or four years
after your master's at twenty-one.

How quickly I run through my little set
of favored pictures . . . pictures starved to words.
My memory economizes so prodigally
I know I have suffered theft.

You did miracles I blushed to acknowledge,
outlines for novels more salable than my poems,
my ambiguities lost seven cities down.
*Roget's* synonyms studded your spoken and written word.

Our days of the great books, scraping and Roman mass –
your confessions had such a vocabulary
you were congratulated by the priests –
I pretended my impatience was concision.

Tortoise and hare
cross the same finishing line –
we learn the spirit is very willing to give up,
but the body is not weak and will not die.

You have spoken so many words and well,
being a woman and you . . . someone must still hear
whatever I have forgotten
or never heard, being a man.

# Since 1939

We missed the declaration of war,
we were on our honeymoon train west;
we leafed through the revolutionary thirties'
*Poems* of Auden, till our heads fell down
swaying with the comfortable
ungainly gait of obsolescence . . .
I miss more things now,
am more consciously mistaken.
I see another girl reading Auden's last book.
She must be very modern,
she dissects him in the past tense.

He is historical now as Munich,
and grew perhaps
to love the rot of capitalism.

We still live
with the devil of his derelictions
he wished to disdain
in the mischievous eccentricity of age.

In our unfinished revolutionary now,
everything seems to end and nothing to begin . . .
The Devil has survived his hollow obits,
and hobbles cursing to his demolition,
a moral heaviness no scales can weigh –
a regurgitation like spots
of yellow buttercups . . .

England like America has lasted
long enough to fear its past,
the habits squashed like wax,
the gay, the prosperous,
their acid of outrage . . .

A decade or so ago,
cavalier African blacks piled
their small English cemetery and dump
to suffocation with statues,
Victorias, Kitcheners, Belfast mercenaries
drained white by rule and carved in soap . . .
caught by the marked cards that earned their keep –
the sovereign misfortune to surpass.

Did they put on too much color like a great actress
for the fulfillment of the dress rehearsal . . .
Did they think they still lived,
if their spirit carried on?

We feel the machine slipping from our hands,
as if someone else were steering;
if we see a light at the end of the tunnel,
it's the light of an oncoming train.

# Endings

*for Harriet Winslow*

The leap from three adjectives to an object
is impossible –

*legs purple and white*
*like purple grapes on marble.*

The change was surprising though laughable
in the 24 years since my first childish
visit to you in Washington –
my foot now touched the first rung of the ladder,
the sharpest pencil line,    ·
far from my Potomac School, my ABC's
with Miss Locke and Miss Gay.

Our arms reached out to each other
too full of drinks . . .
You joked of your blackouts,
your abstractions,
comic and monumental
even for Washington.
You woke wondering why
you woke in another room,
you woke close to drowning.
Effects are without cause;
your doctors found nothing.
A month later you were paralyzed
and never unknotted . . .

A small spark tears at my head,
a flirting of light brown specks in the sky,
explosive pinpricks,
an unaccountable lapse of time.

When I close my eyes, the image is too real,
the solid colors and perspective of life . . .
the tree night-silvered above a bay becomes
the great globe itself, an eye deadened to royal blue
and buried in a jacket of oak leaves.

Why plan; when we stop?

The wandering virus never surmounts the cluster
it never joined.

My eyes flicker, the immortal
is scraped unconsenting from the mortal.